The Heart Manifesto

How to Master the Law of Attraction to Create the Life You Want

Keith Corbett

Empowerment Publishers

Newcastle-Under-Lyme, United Kingdom

Keith Corbett
66 King St, Newcastle-under-Lyme
Staffordshire ST5 1JB, United Kingdom
info@empowermentpublishers.com
http://www.EmpowermentPublishers.com

ISBN-10: 0993182704
ISBN-13: 978-0993182709

Limits of Liability and Disclaimer of Warranty

The author and publisher shall not be liable for your misuse of this material. This book is strictly for informational and educational purposes.

Warning – Disclaimer

The purpose of this book is to educate and entertain. The author and/or publisher do not guarantee that anyone following these techniques, suggestions, tips, ideas, or strategies will become successful. The author and/or publisher shall have neither liability nor responsibility to anyone with respect to any loss or damage caused, or alleged to be caused, directly or indirectly by the information contained in this book.

This book is not intended for use as a source of legal, business, accounting or financial advice. All readers are advised to seek services of competent professionals in legal, business, accounting, and finance field.

In practical advice books, like anything else in life, there are no guarantees of income made. Readers are cautioned to rely on their own judgment about their individual circumstances to act accordingly. . .

Free Gift

As a thank-you for taking the time to read this book I am offering a special bonus: The **HEART Manifesto Power Pack**. It includes an hour-long or so video tutorial, a transcript, an additional resources guide and a workbook to help you create your own **HEART Manifesto** using the process described in Chapter 7.

This normally retails for £197 (approximately $317), which is amazing value in and of itself, but just for buying this book, which can radically change your life for the better all on its own, I am offering it to you absolutely free.

To access the Power Pack go to this web page – http://www.academy4empowerment.com/heart-manifesto - click on "buy now" and when you go to the checkout insert the magical coupon code "manifestnow". This will apply a 100% discount to your purchase.

Dedication

This book is dedicated to awakening entrepreneurs around the world. It's no accident that you're reading this. You know you're here for a reason. It's time to step up, make a difference and achieve the massive success you were born for.

Acknowledgements

To my family and friends who never questioned or seeded doubt toward my incredible journey. Thank you for your loving support.

To the many teachers I sought out over the years who patiently answered my incessant questioning. Your guidance toward my own self-empowerment proved invaluable.

To the authors of the dozens of books I read during my "awakening" phase. I only hope I can inspire others in the way you inspired me.

And not least, to the many clients who gladly volunteered to apply all the crazy exercises I gave you. Your feedback was vital to the development of the **HEART Manifesto**.

About the Author

 Keith Corbett is a master healer, metaphysical researcher and empowerment educator based in Staffordshire, UK and serving clients worldwide.

During his career as a senior PR and marketing manager for a leading technology corporation he learned how to make complex technical information understandable for the average person - "from geek speak to street speak."

Following a series of extraordinary supernatural experiences at the turn of the millennium he embarked on a 15-year odyssey to research and apply metaphysical principles to the real world, culminating in the development of proven, powerful, easy-to-use tools such as the **HEART Manifesto**.

He founded the Academy 4 Empowerment as an informational and educational resource for "awakening entrepreneurs."

Keith is an NLP Master Practitioner, Master of Hypnotherapy, Timeline Therapy Master Practitioner, Spiritual Master Practitioner, Chronic Reversed Polarity Teacher/Practitioner, FreewayCER Tutor/Practitioner, and Reiki Master/Teacher. He also holds a BA Business Studies degree, the CAM Foundation Diploma in Public Relations and the Chartered Institute of Marketing Diploma.

Contents

Introduction

If you know that there is more to the world than meets the eye, but are confused by all the woo-woo mumbo jumbo; if you are wondering whether your life has a purpose and how to find it; if you have tried visualization, affirmations, manifesting techniques and studied The Secret, but the real secret to success still eludes you, then you are in the right place.

Many techniques such as these are only a part of the equation and don't go far enough to really harness the natural laws of the Universe as well as tap into your own Inner Brilliance to create the massive success you were born to enjoy.

It's your birthright and the only thing between you and what you really want is your unconscious programming, which I will show you how to change with the proven principles in this book.

We will start by exploring the "Quantum Field", a subtle, undulating field of energy from which all things emanate, including electricity, magnetism, light and matter itself.

I'll give you scientific, theological and metaphysical evidence of how and why it exists and how to make it work for you. Also, how to use the power of your mind in conjunction with natural laws, and give you some real life examples of how I've done that for myself and my clients to get real-world results.

Then we'll look at what it all means and give you some real insight on how you can use it for yourself, including the real secrets to success that some other resources don't actually tell you.

Most importantly, I'll give you a very powerful tool called the **"HEART Manifesto."** This is a tool you can use on a daily basis to really make these natural processes work for you and create your life on purpose. And I'll show you how to do it with **HEART**; this is the key to success.

And **HEART** is in capital letters because it is a mnemonic - a linguistic device that is both a word in its own right as well as being an anagram. It is the key to unlocking the secrets, which will be revealed in these pages.

So the aim of this book is to empower you to use the natural Laws of the Universe and tap into your own Inner Brilliance to create the life that you want and to help others to do the same. I know, if you're like me, you have a calling to want to make a difference in the world. Only, perhaps as I was some years ago, it isn't quite happening for you.

Most importantly, you'll be more empowered and more awake; you'll be living your life with more of a purpose, and with a greater degree of consciousness.

So in a nutshell, we will examine why most so-called manifesting techniques don't work, we will look at the research project I've done over numerous years to hone it into something very, very effective, demonstrating that this methodology is proven: it is being used successfully every day and you can do the same. I'll show you how to make it work for you.

Bonus

As a thank-you for taking the time to read this book I am offering a special bonus: The **HEART Manifesto Power Pack**. It includes an hour-long or so video tutorial, a transcript, an additional resources guide and a workbook to help you create your own **HEART Manifesto** using the process described in Chapter 7.

This normally retails for £197 (approximately $317), which is amazing value in and of itself, but just for buying this book, which can radically change your life for the better all on its own, I am offering it to you absolutely free.

To access the Power Pack go to this web page – http://www.academy4empowerment.com/heart-manifesto - click on "buy now" and when you go to the checkout insert the magical coupon code "manifestnow". This will apply a 100% discount to your purchase.

My Story

So who am I and what qualifies me to be talking about any of this? Well, I'm the founder of Academy 4 Empowerment, an educational and informational resource designed to empower awakening entrepreneurs to harness the natural laws of the Universe and tap into their own inner brilliance to create the massive success they were born to enjoy.

Also, I'm a Master Healer, meaning that I've got more certifications than I can count, having trained to master or instructor level in many of them during my ongoing search to discover how the Universe really works. I have run a holistic wellness practice for 15 years and am the only European practitioner currently offering healing for Chronic Reversed Polarity.

Some of my certifications include NLP Master Practitioner, Master of Hypnosis, Time Line Therapyr Master Practitioner, FreewayCER Tutor Practitioner, Polarity Balancing Practitioner/Tutor, Master Herbalist, Reiki Master/Teacher, and Spiritual Master Practitioner.

I'm also using techniques such as Ho'oponopono, Higher Self Therapy, Kinesiology, 5-Element Chinese Acupressure, Rossiter Workouts, and a host of other practices that I've found to be useful in getting stellar results for clients.

Why I mention all of this is because once I started in the healing arena I noticed how clients got much more rapid and powerful results when the mind was engaged in the healing process.

This led me to learn about the Law of Attraction and how we are basically "magnets" for whatever is a vibrational match to us. If that sounds a bit far out, stay with me until you've read Chapter 1 at least and you'll perhaps see how it's possible.

This in turn led me to embark on a journey into metaphysical research. I basically went on tons of courses, studied at the feet of gurus and leaders in the field, attended conferences, subscribed to publications, newsletters and online resources. Not to mention reading more books than you can shake a stick at. I couldn't rest until I knew all the secrets of the Universe.

Well, I am still a long way from that goal - I don't believe they are all even knowable by the human mind, but that's a different story. But I have amassed a great deal of knowledge. I understand undoubtedly that knowledge and learnings are only useful if they are applied. So practical application is the core of my research.

For more than a decade I've been particularly interested in understanding how the Universe works, especially the Law of Attraction and to find ways to apply it in the real world. I tried every method and technique I came across, first on myself and then with clients to figure out what works.

When I originally started my holistic practice at the turn of the Millennium, it was as a personal interest "on the side" while still working for a major international corporation. I actually have 30 years' experience in high-tech PR and marketing under my belt.

A skill I honed there was to take complex technical information and boil it down into something like a product description that is concise, compelling and easily understood by customers. From 'geek-speak to street-speak', so to speak.

In more recent years I took the opportunity for voluntary redundancy, gave up the day job and have focused exclusively on all things holistic, applying the learnings I've gained in my own practice, developing myself and helping others to do the same.

In this time I have increased my intuition and my psychic powers quite phenomenally, but stayed very grounded in the real world. In particular, in the process of doing the metaphysical research, I've had some very extraordinary experiences.

These include being visited by the ghost of my deceased Grandmother and receiving a healing for a 20-year old injury that was supposedly incurable. These two things in particular helped me to realize that there is more to the world than meets the eye and started me on this journey of self and Universal discovery. Since then I have had many supernatural experiences, witnessed numerous miraculous healings and know that I really can create my life experience any way I want.

One big observation I have is how so many people disempower themselves and unwittingly play the role of victim, often as a result of their 'programming' from an early age, not realizing the power they have to change that.

I am all about empowerment. I can see the light in people, and folks, it's time to stop hiding this and come out and shine because the world needs us now. The Earth is at a critical juncture in its evolution -- Which way will it go? Into the new age of enlightenment or back into darkness?

It's up to us. I believe I am here at this time to be a healer and teacher to aid this process. If you are reading this, so are you. You feel the truth of it, don't you?

People the world over are waking up to who they really are, are disillusioned with old systems that no longer serve us and are seeking truth. They are looking for torch-bearers to show them the way. That's us folks. It doesn't serve the world for you to hide your light or play small.

So, if you are someone who knows that there is more to the world than meets the eye, and you're looking for practical ways to implement it, especially if you're a coach, therapist, healer or entrepreneur who wants to make a difference in the world, then you are in the right place.

The Missing Pieces

Now, if you have already looked at other 'manifesting' tools and it hasn't worked for you so far, that's because you're missing key information. What I want to do now is fill in the missing pieces to show you how the universe really works.

By applying my skill at transforming complex concepts into easy-to-follow language, combined with years of trying and testing everything I could unearth, I can give you the benefit of this knowledge without having to go through the same arduous journey of discovery that I did.

Perhaps you are reading this book because you sense there is something to it, even if you have tried any of the plethora of manifesting methods that abound in the self-help and new age fields, but have struggled to get them to work so far on anything of significance.

The reason it hasn't worked for you so far may just be down to a lack of understanding of the mechanics of the Universe (that is, until reading this book) and your own unconscious programming that has installed limiting beliefs that you are not even consciously aware of.

Maybe you've tried affirmations, visualizations, vision boards, meditations, spells and so on. But they're only part of the story. Perhaps you don't believe it's possible, but your beliefs **do** shape your reality: I will demonstrate that.

Now, some folk could have other mental or emotional blocks that might be getting in your way, and a key thing to know is that behaviors are often unconscious; you may not even know you have them. I will show you, at the end, a way you can get any unconscious blocks and beliefs released so that you will be free to move forward in the way that you would like.

So how is it possible to master the Law of Attraction and actually create your life exactly the way would want it? I will show you in these pages scientific, theological and metaphysical evidence that will demonstrate exactly why that's doable. Then give you a proven, powerful tool to do it for yourself.

It is deceptively simple because I've boiled out all the complexity to deliver just the salient facts to give you what you need. Just like you don't need to understand internal combustion engines to drive a car. So read on to truly understand how to master the Law of Attraction.

Chapter 1: The Quantum Field

The first thing I'd like to talk about is the Quantum Field. This has been called many things, such as the Zero Point Field, Universal Energy and the Akashik Field, but I like the name Quantum Field, so for our purposes we'll stick with that.

It's universal energy, a field of potentiality, impacted by human intention, whether that intention is conscious or unconscious. So what does that actually mean?

Well, for example, if you were to build a scale model of an atom, you could go to your nearest major football stadium, take a garden pea and put it on the centre circle, and that would represent the nucleus of the atom. Now, in scale terms, if you then went to the uppermost stand, outermost seat, in the farthest corner of the stadium, and put a cotton bud on the seat there, that would represent the closest electron to the nucleus in that atom.

So what's holding it together? What's between it? Basically, it's all energy. There are many texts on this topic, but I am going to just introduce you to a couple of authors I particularly like who have described it well.

Gregg Braden

The first is Gregg Braden, a New York Times bestselling author with 37 books in 22 languages. He is an internationally renowned pioneer in bridging science to ancient wisdom and the real world. He's a former geologist and computer systems designer for major corporations, and he gives a great description of the Quantum Field in his book called *The Divine Matrix*[1], which was published in 2007.

He calls it "**a field of energy that unites all creation, where every part is connected to every other. It communicates through the language of emotion**." What I like about his works is that he bases them on study and investigation in the real world, like myself. So this is a mumbo-jumbo-free zone.

Wayne Dyer

Another author I quite like is Wayne Dyer, who talks also about a similar sort of thing. Again, he's an internationally renowned author, speaks in the field of self-development. He's got over 30 books, and has created many audio programs, videos and the like. He has a doctorate in Educational Counselling from Wayne State University, and all kinds of credentials. One book in particular I like of his is called, *Stop the Excuses: How to Change Lifelong Thoughts*[2].

He points out that we live in a universe that is all energy. Our physical universe and everything in it is a vibrating machine: everything vibrates and the frequency of those vibrations determines how everything appears, including our body, which senses our thoughts and has energy components that can be measured.

One of the key things Dr Dyer points out is that he says he has **"the power to harmonize with the vibrational source and can activate whatever I focus on"**. He believes that this ability is within everybody, focusing on what you want activates this, and anyone can do it.

Pam Grout

Another author I would just like to include in this section is Pam Grout. She is not quite as well known as the other two, but authored a pretty cool book called *E-Squared*[3], which went viral: it was marketed entirely through social media. What I liked about it was that it had some very practical research exercises in it.

I'll give you a quick example of one of them, which she calls the 'Dude Abides Principle', which is basically a way to test that the Quantum Field actually exists. She said, give it a test: "within 48 hours, give me a free gift". So, I though, I'll do that exercise.

Funnily enough, the next day I went to a networking meeting and the presenter was a person who does horoscopes and they said "If you buy my book, I'll give you a free horoscope reading". Well, I always buy the presenter's books when I go to these meetings, and I wasn't expecting a free horoscope reading, but I did get that, so I took that as an unexpected free gift.

You could argue I would have got that anyway, that it is just a coincidence of timing, but there are so many synchronicities that there just has to be something to it, as I will explain later.

Pam Grout has another exercise where she will have you looking for things, such as green cars, for example. So, we decided to try that one summer's day. My son and I were having a drive down a country road in Wales and we said "let's see how many green cars we can spot, because we haven't seen any lately". Well, in 20 minutes, we saw 47 green cars. Funnily enough, we hadn't noticed any until that time. My son said to me "this is too easy, let's do orange cars".

℣ 18

Incredibly, at the next junction, there were **four** orange cars; two on each side. Not only that, but when we came a T-junction, we were sitting there waiting to pull out and what goes past? A delivery van that is green and orange! Okay, maybe it's coincidence and maybe it would have happened anyway, but, it's interesting, isn't it?

Incredibly interesting as they are, these anecdotes don't really prove anything on their own, so in the next chapter I aim to provide solid scientific evidence for the existence of the Quantum Field and that it responds to human intention.

Chapter 2: Scientific Evidence

So, let's get on to the scientific evidence for the Quantum Field. These are real world experiments done by genuine academics and scientists who know what they're talking about. There has been many, many studies on this, and I'm just presenting here some of my favorite ones. Some are quite well known and established, some are not so much, but just as profound.

John Wheeler

The first person I want to introduce you to in this section is John Wheeler, who actually coined the phrase 'the Quantum Field'. He is a Princeton University physicist, a friend of Albert Einstein, and he revived interest in General Relativity after the Second World War.

He tried to achieve Einstein's vision of a Unified Field Theory and popularized some terms like 'black hole', 'quantum foam', and 'worm hole', which are used quite commonly today. Many of his students have contributed to quantum mechanics and gravitational research and knowledge.

One of the key things that this eminent, respected scientist summarized, from all his years of work, is that **"we are not observers but participators in the universe"**. That's a very, very key point.

James Clerk Maxwell

The next person I would like to mention is James Clerk Maxwell, a Scottish Nobel Prize Winner for Electromagnetic Theory, all the way back in the 19th century. He published *A Dynamical Theory of the Electromagnetic Field*[4] in 1865. This is known as the second great unification in physics, after the first realized by Isaac Newton, which laid the foundation for such fields as special relativity and quantum mechanics.

Maxwell was in fact voted third most important physicist of all time, after Einstein and Newton. One of the things he is most well-known for is formulating a set of equations that describe electricity, magnetism and optics, as **"manifestation of the same phenomenon: namely, the magnetic field. Electricity, magnetism and even light, all manifest from it"**.

Max Planck

Moving on to Max Planck, who is quite well known as the father of quantum physics. A German theoretical physicist who originated Quantum Theory, he won the Nobel Prize for physics in 1918 and revolutionized human understanding of atomic and subatomic processes.

The key conclusion that he arrived in his lifetime of cutting edge scientific work was: "**we must assume a conscious and intelligent mind is behind it**". It is beyond the scope of this book to expand on that particular point, but I just thought that was a very interesting observation. The main point is that this world-leading physicist is supporting the idea of a Unifying Field or a Quantum Field.

Geoffrey Ingram Taylor

Now onto Sir Geoffrey Ingram Taylor, a British physicist, mathematician and expert on fluid dynamics and wave theory.

He is regarded as one of the most notable scientists of the 20th Century and did much research around what is known as the "double slit" experiment.

This originated from a chap called Young but it was Taylor who developed it and really researched it quite thoroughly, and he found that this whole things works with a single sub-atomic particle, such as a photon.

In 1909, his first paper on Quanta proved that matter and energy can display characteristics of both classically defined waves and particles. So it's both energy and matter: it can be either.

Taylor showed that an electron particle, as well as being one of the tiniest physical particles, also behaves as a wave form and reacts to observers' knowledge. What his team found was that they got different results according to the expectations of the experimenter. So, what they are thinking influences the outcome of the experiment.

He said that "**the collapse of the quantum wave function brings reality into existence**", in other words the conscious observation by a person brings matter into existence from energy, and he proved that repeatedly in his work. Humans are creating reality with their minds!

Bruce Lipton

Now I'd like to introduce Bruce Lipton, PhD, who is a cell biologist. A former medical school professor and research scientist, he eventually resigned from teaching to further his education and research in this area because he realized that the conventional teachings that he was required to convey to his students were seriously off the mark from what he knew to be the truth.

He teaches that life is not controlled by genes, but that there is

an invisible formless energy that constitutes a gene's environment, which is the architect of life. He showed that your personal belief system trumps your DNA: your beliefs control your biology.

This actually revolutionized our understanding of the link between mind and matter, and the profound effects on our personal lives, and the collective life. So basically we can control our lives by controlling our perception, and he is the academic who proved that. You can read his story for yourself in his best-selling book *The Biology of Belief*[5].

Ervin Lazlo

Now, I'd like to introduce Ervin Lazlo, who is not quite as famous as some as the other people I've covered so far, but is very contemporary. He's received the highest degree in Philosophy and Human Sciences from the Sorbonne, the University of Paris, and a coveted artist's diploma of the Liszt Ferenz Academy of Budapest.

He has four honorary doctorates at Yale, Princeton, Euston, Portland, North West Universities in the fields of Philosophy and System Sciences. He has been twice nominated for the Nobel Peace Prize.

He was also awarded the Japanese Peace prize and has authored more than 70 books. One of his books that I really like, because he puts it in real layperson's language, which means even I can understand it, is called *Science and the Akashic Field*[6].

He's talking about the same thing that we are referring to - the Quantum Field. There's an interconnecting cosmic field at the roots of reality which conserves and conveys information. He's done studies into vacuum physics which show that it is real and underlies space itself. And to quote him: "**from a subtle sea of undulating energies, all things emanate**." I find that fascinating.

Konstantin Korotkov

The next person I'd like to mention is Konstantin Korotkov, who is also still practicing today. He's a professor of physics at St. Petersburg State Technical University and he particularly looks into the area of bio-field research, which studies the effects of the human mind, thoughts and energy, on our surrounding environment.

He's done research into mind/matter interaction at Princeton University as well. He's published over 200 papers in leading journals in physics and biology, and owns 17 patents on biophysics inventions. He has also authored nine books.

He says "**we're developing the idea that our consciousness is part of the material world, and that with our consciousness, we can directly influence our world**." He essentially talks about the effects of the mind's intention on the physical world.

In one experiment, he used a random generator machine to mimic a coin flip. Left to its own devices, the machine eventually comes up 50/50; half of the time it would be heads, and the other half it would be tails. But when people were brought into the equation, they could influence it to such an extent that "**contemporary physics is unable to explain what is actually happening**." Basically, people can change the world simply by using their own energy and minds.

Poponin and Gariaev

In 1990 Hungarian scientists Poponin and Gariaev of the Russian Academy of Sciences in Moscow discovered a phenomenon called the phantom effect of DNA as a surprise effect during experiments measuring the vibrational modes of DNA in solution using a sophisticated and expensive laser photon correlation spectrometer (LPCS).

In an eight-year long study of the subtle energy fields of human DNA and biology, they concluded that **everything is made of photons** and that **"human DNA has a direct effect on photon particles"**.

Military Experiments

US army experiments in the '90s, in Colorado showed that human emotion has a direct influence on DNA and the way cells function. They hooked subjects up to machines to measures their physiological responses to images they showed them; serene pictures, horrific pictures, and all kinds of things, and showed how their cells reacted to that.

And they also took a swab of cells from inside their mouth, put them in a petri dish in another room, hooked them up, and found that as the person that the cells came from was experiencing physiological reactions, those separated cells reacted in exactly the same way, even though they were detached.

They even put them in a truck and drove them 350 miles away up to Wyoming, and they found that it was not affected by distance. Isn't that interesting?

Institute of Heartmath

The Institute of Heartmath in the US conducts research into this field and they have found that our DNA gives us access to the energy that connects the universe, and that **"emotion is the key to tapping into the field"**. That reinforces some of the things we've already seen earlier.

Bruce Moseley

Dr. Bruce Moseley, from the Bayer School of Medicine, published a study in the New England Journal of Medicine back in 2002. He's a knee surgeon, and he did a study where they divided his patients into three groups.

In one of them, they actually shaved the cartilage, which is what the patients came in for. The second group, they just flushed out the joint, but without actually doing any more work in the knee. And on the third group, they did a fake surgery, so they didn't get anything at all, just thought that they did.

What they found was that all three groups improved by the same amount, and he concluded "**my skill as a surgeon had no benefit on those patients. The net benefit for osteoarthritis of the knee was the placebo effect**". How interesting is that?

One placebo group member, Tim Perez, walked with a cane before having fake surgery, and afterwards he was playing basketball with his grandchildren.

It's all in the mind!

Albert Einstein

Finally in this chapter, I want to reference the great man himself, probably the best known scientific mind that ever lived on this planet - Albert Einstein. His famous equation, which every school kid knows, or perhaps should know, is **E=MC2**.

But what is this actually saying? I have often wondered. In this equation, E stands for Energy, M is Mass (that's solid stuff to you and me) and C is a Constant, which in this case is actually the speed of light. So Energy equals Mass multiplied by the Speed of Light squared.

Now, this is an equation, so what's on one side of the equation is the same as what's on the other side of it. So, what he's basically saying is that **mass is energy** and he can prove that mathematically. We are, in fact, all energy. So is everything else that exists. Isn't that interesting? And we've known it for so long!

I find it incredible that key physics concepts such as these are taught in schools, but that the real implications of them - that we influence reality with our energy and thoughts - is somehow missed.

These days it is thought that science and religion don't have much in common, but in the next chapter I want to briefly explore how some of the world's major religions are in agreement with what our leading scientists have been saying here.

Chapter 3: Theological Evidence

What I'd like to show here is that ancient teachings from different religions actually have similar underpinnings. Any differences are mainly manmade, dogmatic things that have developed in different regions in different ways.

Basically, there's quite a lot of religious and theological evidence to support the idea of a Quantum Field and that human thought shapes reality.

Buddhism

For example, in Mahayana Buddhism, they say **"what is reality, and what you perceive as reality, is one and the same"**. They say that reality can only exist where our mind creates a focus, which is pretty much supporting what we've found in the scientific realm: our modern scientists are now proving the same thing that the Buddha taught centuries before.

The Bible

In the bible, you may have heard of the expression "ask, and you shall receive", well, that was actually a condensed phrase in the King James edition. Thankfully, with the discovery of the Dead Sea scrolls, we actually have the original scripture available to us now.

What that passage actually says is **"ask without hidden motive, and be surrounded by your answer. Be enveloped by what you desire that your gladness be full."** Notice how it says "without hidden motive," which gives us a clue as to one of the keys to successful manifesting. More on that later.

This I got from a book called *Prayers of the Cosmos: Meditations on the Aramaic Words of Jesus*[7] by Neil Douglas-Klotz. It's quite an interesting text.

The teachings of Jesus allude to the Law of Attraction in many ways, including this one: "a**s you wish that others would do to you, do so to them**" (Luke 6.31). This is the "do unto others as you would be done to" principle, also known as "what goes around comes around" in modern parlance.

I interpret it to mean that if you are good to others - and if you read the complete text you'll see he means all others, not just friends and family (i.e. love your enemy) - then others will be good to you. Like attracts like!

Tibetan Monks

In another one of Gregg Braden's books called *The Isaiah Effect*[8] he talks about visiting a monastery in Tibet, and asks them what they're doing when they're doing all their praying, chanting and so on.

The monks said that they are trying to create the feeling that what they are praying for already is. And not just any feeling, but doing it without ego or judgment to the extent that "**the stronger our desire to change the world, the more elusive it becomes**" because that desire is ego-based.

Another key point they make is that you must have the feeling of abundance and peace as if they have already happened. In there, we've got some real key pointers; feeling without ego or judgment, and as if it's already happened. These give us further big clues as to how we might leverage these powers for our own use.

Vedic Tradition

Going onto the Vedic tradition and the teachings ascribed to the Lord Krishna - to quote, **"all that we are is the result of what we have thought"**. So this is reinforcing the idea that what we think creates our reality.

They also say that **"one should perform karma with nonchalance, without expecting the benefits, because sooner or later, one shall definitely get the fruits"**. So, again, it's very similar to the passage from the bible, in that the lack of expectation and not being attached to the outcome, is the way to get it.

They also teach that **"if one speaks or acts with a pure thought, happiness follows one like a shadow that never leaves"**. And, that, again, is very, very interesting when you break it down.

I'll show you later on how we can apply these principles.

Chapter 4: Metaphysical Evidence

I'd like to move on into a little section now on metaphysical evidence. 'Metaphysical' just means 'beyond the physical' - so it's not something that you can necessarily perceive with your five senses, but is no less real.

In the metaphysical traditions of the world, the idea of the quantum field is prevalent. In the mystery schools of Ancient Greece, they talk of Ether, the Vedic traditions talk about Prana, in the Orient there's Chi or Ki, and even native traditions such as the Native Americans talk about the Great Spirit; this underlying energy that pervades throughout all of our reality.

Neville

The first person I'd like to introduce you to in this field is Neville Goddard, who normally just went by Neville. A mystic hailing from Barbados, he was a prominent figure in the New Thought Movement of the 1950's who gained recognition as a famous miraculous healer and philosophical speaker.

In his book *The Power of Awareness*[10], which is a really, really good read, he says **"everything done to us or by us is a product of our consciousness and nothing else. Our imagination creates reality."** He actually turned around some terminal illness cases (i.e. healed people who were dying), just by showing them the bigger picture, as he puts it. And that is, that consciousness creates.

The key is persisting in the assumption that your desire is already fulfilled, and your world inevitably conforms to that assumption. So, **"imagination creates reality. Make your**

future dream a present fact". And we thank him for bringing that to our attention.

Rhonda Byrne

Rhonda Byrne is responsible for bringing the movie and book called *The Secret*[11] to the masses. Now, as you may have guessed, I do not think that it is complete enough to be a powerful manifesting tool. It is good, as far as it goes, but it just doesn't go far enough in my view.

When it first came out I took a good look at it, being quite interested in this field of research and said to myself then that I didn't think people would get consistent results using just the visualization techniques that it promotes.

Sure enough, that is what I heard from clients and others when they said they had tried using its methods. Some met with some success of course, but most of the time it would end in disappointment.

However, that said, it does contain some real nuggets that are useful to include in a more comprehensive program of manifesting. What The Secret does say is that any words that you speak have a frequency, and the moment you speak them, they're released into the universe. **The Law of Attraction responds to all frequencies, and so it's also responding to the words that you speak.**

So when you use very strong words, like 'terrible, 'shocking' and 'horrible' to describe any situation in your life, you're actually sending out an equally strong frequency and the Law of Attraction must respond by bringing that frequency back to you. The law is actually impersonal, it just simply matches your frequency.

❧ 32

So, as she says, "**do you see how important it is for you to speak strongly about what you want and not to use strong words about what you don't want**". So, words have power, folks, you may have heard that, and Rhonda Byrne certainly is a believer.

I am, too, and I'll show you how to use words to good effect shortly.

Esther Hicks

Now I'd like to talk a little about Esther Hicks - she's a 'channel' for a non-physical being called Abraham. You may be familiar with channeling, or you may not.

Personally, I don't really worry too much about where the information comes from. What I'm interested in: is it empowering and useful? Can I use it in the real world? I'll take on board what they say, I'll try it out, and if it works, I'll incorporate it. If it doesn't work for me, then maybe I'll leave it, but maybe it'll work for someone else, who knows?

Basically, Abraham talks a lot about the Law of Attraction, explaining that it's simply 'like attracts like'. And what they say is, when thoughts are focused, you'll access more of what you're thinking about. You don't attract what you desire, you attract what you are.

So again, this is more about not being so attached to the outcome, and to being it rather than wanting it. Another things they say, which I think is very, very important, and you certainly don't get this in *The Secret*, is: **"It is the action you take today that ties you to the future event"**.

Wallace Wattles

Just to reinforce that point, we'll come on to Wallace Wattles, who was the author of *The Science of Getting Rich*[11], originally published in 1910. You can actually get it for free on the internet today and I have put a link to it in the bibliography at the back of this book.

Mr. Wattles came from a very poor background with little or no education and actually ended up quite well off by applying the principles that he teaches in the book. One of the key points he makes is **"every day, take every reasonable step towards your goal"**. So that's reinforcing the importance of taking action in the real world. You can't just 'ohm' things into existence.

Another thing he said, which I thought was quite interesting, was that **"your desires are to be delivered through the everyday machinations of the world"**. What's interesting about that is, when I've applied the principles and actually been successful in achieving something or getting something manifested, it's almost as if it was in process for many years before I even thought of it.

It makes the mind boggle when I kind of wonder, would it have happened anyways? Who knows? What I do know is, as long as I apply the right principles, I get the results. More on that later.

Another thing Wattles said is that most people won't have the mental fortitude to do this, meaning the conscious brain work required to visualize and manifest what they want. And I do

have to say, that it does take a lot of effort to do it the way he teaches, in terms of holding the thoughts about what you want consistently for long periods of time.

Happily, through further research, I've actually found a way around that, so when I come to show you the tool in a little while, you'll understand that you don't actually need to have as much brain power as you might have done in 1910 using the Wattles method to achieve the same or even better results.

Napoleon Hill

Napoleon Hill is the author of probably the world's best-selling personal development book of all time, called *Think and Grow Rich*[12]. Published originally in 1937, it has sold more than 20 million copies.

The industrialist Andrew Carnegie set him the task to go and talk to all of the most successful people in America, including hugely successful business leaders such as Henry Ford, to basically see what makes them tick, what characteristics or methods they had for attracting great wealth and to put it all together into a book.

He did a lot of examining of the power of personal beliefs and the role they play in personal success. He quickly identified this as the way to get success: "**believe that you can be successful**".

He became an advisor to U.S. president Franklin D. Roosevelt, and looked a lot into how achievement actually occurs, creating a formula for it that puts considerable financial success in reach of the average person. These were the focal points of his books.

Basically he says "**any idea, plan or purpose may be placed in the mind through repetition of thought**," and also, "**what the mind of man can conceive and believe, it can achieve.**" That's one of his hallmark expressions.

What I liked about it is that he's not just making stuff up; he's a regular guy who's gone out and researched it and found the answers. Another things he says that I find really interesting is, **"cherish your visions and your dreams, as they are the children of your soul, the blueprints of your ultimate achievements"**. So your vision and dreams become your reality; how interesting is that?

Nikos Kazantzakis

The next person I'd like to discuss is not quite as well known: Nikos Kazantzakis. He wrote the book *Zorba the Greek,*[13] which was turned into a movie featuring the great actor Anthony Quinn in 1964 – I think it's actually a great film and Quinn plays it beautifully.

Nikos was a truly passionate man and passion, for him, was a key thing in his life. He said **"by believing passionately in something that does not yet exist, we can create it,"** and **"in order to succeed, we must first believe that we can"**.

So, there's another philosopher who found the power of belief in succeeding to create what we want. Another thing he said, which I also found interesting, is that **"the nonexistent is whatever we have not sufficiently desired"**. So having the desire is also very important - if your heart isn't in it, then you may find it harder to come by.

Carl Jung

Carl Young, a little bit more famous, was a contemporary to the father of modern psychotherapy, Sigmund Freud. A Swiss psychiatrist and psychotherapist, Jung founded 'analytic psychology' and coined many phrases used commonly today such as 'the collective unconscious', 'dream analysis', and 'synchronicity'.

One of the concepts that he is most well-known for is that of **'perception is projection'**. What that means is, what you're perceiving in your outer world is actually a projection of your inner consciousness.

So, when an inner situation is not made conscious, it appear consciously as 'fate', which leaves you wondering why certain things are happening to you, while not being aware that you're actually creating them yourself.

Another thing that he popularized is the idea of 'individuation', where integrating the opposites, including the conscious with the unconscious, whilst still maintaining their relative autonomy, was the way to actually be more in control of what you're projecting.

And he considered it to be the central process of human development. A very wise man. Through years of study myself, I have become acutely aware of how the Unconscious Mind presents challenges as a 'message' for us to become consciously aware that something requires our attention.

This can manifest in many ways, such as emotional or physical pain, relationship issues, problems with career, neighbors, finances and particularly health.

Fortunately the process works well in the other direction as well - the unconscious readily takes instruction from the conscious mind when we seed it with positive ideas about what we truly desire.

Maharishi Effect

The Maharishi Effect is named after the Maharishi Yogi, a big proponent of meditation. In 1972 a group of meditators went round 24 US cities at different times, different lunar cycles, in different seasons and they just meditated to reduce the crime rate. Incredibly, they actually did it. It was documented with and statistically significantly results to prove that this was an intervention that worked.

International Peace Project

In the 1980s there was an international peace project in the Middle East, where they used transcendental meditation to try and achieve peace, and that had a definite effect on the hostilities that were going on there at the time as well.

Quite interestingly, what we find from these studies is, that the minimum number of people required to jump start a change in consciousness is only the square root of 1% of a population.

So for example, if the population of the UK, where I live, is about 62 million, it just needs 787 people to jumpstart a change in consciousness. In the US, where there are around 310 million people, it's only going to need about 1,700 to do that.

We've got nearly 7 billon people on the planet in total, so only a little over 8,000 would be needed to activate an increase in human consciousness on Earth! That's quite doable, is it not?

Beijing Clinic

Another example that I found really interesting involves a clinic in Beijing, China where a female patient had a life threatening inoperable mass in her bladder. The healers there were just doing a chant of 'already healed' and the tumor shrank and disappeared in only four minutes. There is actually a video on the Internet where you can see it happening on the screen of an ultrasound machine.

The Three Minds

The Three Minds is a concept I first came across in 2004 on a CD that was distributed with a magazine I bought. I encountered it several times since and it came up as a core model for how the mind works on a spiritual seminar I attended.

This prompted further analysis and I find it to be a very useful construct when applied to manifesting methodologies.

The concept is derived from Huna shamanism - the ancient native spiritual tradition of Hawaii. In the illustration here you can see a representation of the three minds. In the middle, you have your conscious mind; this is what you use every day to make decisions with and to go out and look at the world with. The conscious mind is really based on logic, but also on separation. It's what keeps you perceiving yourself as an individual.

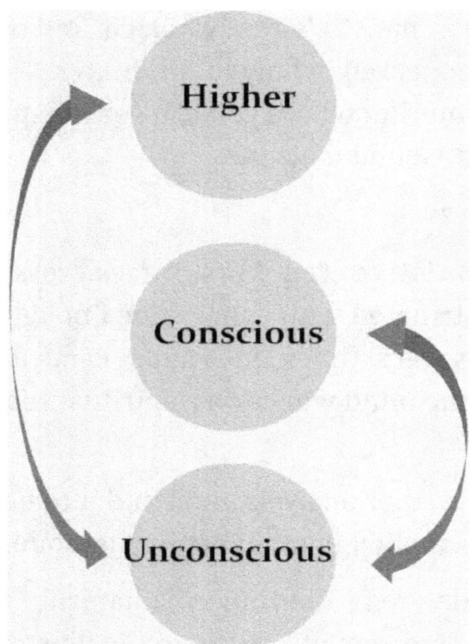

Below that we can see the unconscious mind, often called the subconscious, and this is the seat of all your behaviors, emotions and personality, but also it is really about connectedness.

The unconscious mind can actually perceive the connection to everybody that we all have. It's also known as the dream weaver, because this is where your dreams get created as it interprets the communications from the higher mind, often called the higher self, or the part of you that is really connected to all-that-is or source energy.

If you want to go this route, you could call the higher mind 'the spark of divinity' within the individual. It transcends time and space, is infinite and holographic - essentially where everything actually is one.

It knows you are perfect, can remove problems and create everything you ask for; it creates your universe. Now, if that's so, you may be tempted to ask "why don't we just ask the higher mind for what we want and get it right away then?"

Look closer at the illustration again and you will see that the conscious and unconscious minds are communicating with one another, represented by the arrows, and the higher mind and the unconscious mind are communicating with one another, but there's no direct communication between the conscious and the higher.

So you have to go through the unconscious mind. And none of these things speak English or Sanskrit or Hebrew or anything else - they use symbolism. So; feelings and images, things like that are the way we get the messages.

Also, the unconscious mind is where all our beliefs, emotions and behaviors emanate, which makes it a sort of filter. That's why, when I work directly with clients we do so much work on the unconscious mind, enabling good conscious-unconscious rapport to access useful information and change the negative programming into positive.

We are naught but the product of our programming and much of it is unconscious, accepted by us as a result of experiences and messages adopted from parents, teachers, peers, television and a host of sources.

If a person is really stuck and can't make the progress they desire whatever they try, it is inevitably going to be due to some kind of block at the level of the unconscious mind, which needs to be dug out.

Cause and Effect

Cause and effect is another popular phrase used in therapy circles. When we understand these concepts, it gives an opportunity to be 'at cause' rather than 'at effect' in our lives.

By recognizing that you are causing what's going on in your life, that's the key to empowerment. If you're playing the role of victim, and perceiving yourself to be at the effect of external circumstances, that's disempowering.

Being at cause means taking responsibility for your own life experience and knowing that if you're not happy with it you have the power to change it. Only you can change it. Making excuses for why things aren't going your way is totally giving up your power.

Now that you know you have it, there is no escaping the responsibility any more. So, you have the power. There's enough evidence here to demonstrate that, and you will find the links to research it further for yourself if you're still not convinced.

"The power of human thought, or human intention, is definitely one of the most powerful forces in the universe."

The Law of Attraction

Law of Attraction (LOA) is a popular term today, but what does it really mean? So here is the executive summary - the LOA is one of the 'immutable' laws of the Universe that works on the principle of 'like attracts like'.

Immutable means it is permanent, fixed, can't be changed. That's good news for us because once we understand how to work it, it works brilliantly. Consistent, repeatable results is what we want - and that is what we get.

So how does it work? Well, I think I have sufficiently demonstrated so far that all matter is in fact energy. Everything is energy. Just vibrating at different rates, or frequencies. It is our mind, through the faculty of our five physical-plane senses that interprets things as solid or 'real'.

We know that all things emanate from the Quantum Field and that it communicates through the language of emotion. We also know that our mental/emotional states affect our physical body as well as our energy body.

For more on this, go to the Free Stuff page on my website - http://academy4empowerment.com/free-stuff/ - and watch the free video tutorial called, *Your Energy Body*.

So all of our emotions, behaviors, thoughts and beliefs, whether conscious or unconscious, combine to create an energetic frequency or 'vibration' that we resonate to. And we will attract to us anything that we are a vibrational match for.

Therefore, the trick is to be a match for what you want. How many people do you know who focus on what they don't want, complain about everything and end up getting more things to complain about?

So, how does it benefit us to know all this stuff? I continue to ask myself this question and look for new ways to test and apply the concepts in the real world.

The next chapter summarizes some of the experiences I've had on this journey. In it I'll explain a bit about how I applied my research in real-world examples and learned how to set up the appropriate vibration to get the LOA working for you.

Chapter 5: Research

Now, I did say I've been researching and practicing this for over a decade at the time of writing. In this time I have developed a proven methodology to make this knowledge work for me and for others. Here are a couple of personal examples.

In 2005 I had spent the previous eight years living the US with my work and I was then returning to the U.K. I was living in Colorado, which is a lovely place, but unfortunately real estate values had stayed pretty flat in the time I was there, whereas in the UK they had skyrocketed to the point where it didn't look as though we would be able to afford to buy the kind of house we had lived in before we left.

House

So, I decided to apply the principles I had learned. I was very detailed about what I wanted in a home – four bedrooms, detached house, in a village, in the countryside, up a hill, with a drive and gates, and in a particular school district, within budget.

Lo and behold, when we got to the U.K., there was a guy who had split up with his partner and had reduced the price of his property quite considerably. He would only allow people to view it who were in a position to buy (i.e. had no chain or house of their own to sell), which was us.

His criteria of a prospective purchaser were so restrictive that we must have been about the only people who met it at that time. Our criteria were so specific, especially the budget part, that this house was about the only one that met it. A perfect match!

It ticked all of the boxes for what I had set my intention on and so we were able to get a substantial discount and afford a property that perfectly met our needs, which would have otherwise seemed unaffordable. Interesting "coincidence," wasn't it?

Car

Also, I'd sold my motor vehicle in the U.S. and wanted to buy a car in the U.K. using the same money. Basically, I didn't want to spend any more on the British car than I'd received in payment for my used U.S. vehicle, but as some people know, things in the U.K. tend to be somewhat more expensive than things in the U.S.

I wanted a car I could get the whole family, the dog, and the luggage in if we wanted to go away for the weekend, for example. I quite fancied a green car (I see green as a healing color), I wanted to have wood effect trim on the inside, and regular analog dials rather than computerized digital displays, because I'm a bit of a traditionalist at heart in some ways - despite, or perhaps because of spending my corporate life in the high-tech industry.

I had no idea how I could afford such a thing, but nonetheless I put these principles to work, and when I got back to the U.K. I found that the year before, the car company Rover had gone out of business – just through bad management really – and they had pre-registered a lot of cars in order to try and inflate their market share figures.

So there were a lot of Rovers that had just sat on car parks for 12 months, and I was able to get one. It was a 12-month old car with 7 miles on the clock, and at half of its original list price. Now, did my doing a manifesting technique cause Rover to go bust? No, of course not. My desires just materialized through the normal machinations of the world. Interestingly enough, I got what I wanted.

Business

I applied this also to starting my holistic business. I had stayed in the corporate world longer than I wanted to because I had an unconscious limiting belief that I couldn't make a living doing holistic work on my own.

Once I had that identified and released by a fellow practitioner, I was able to move forward and start building my practice. Clients started coming out of the woodwork from the most unexpected of places. Also, what a 'coincidence' that as soon as I decided to apply the manifesting principles I had learned, a voluntary redundancy program with a healthy severance package was announced. I applied, was accepted and got a decent capital injection to get my self-employed life off to a good start.

Retirement Plan

Another personal example, was a retirement plan. Now, I worked for a good company for a good amount of time, albeit in different countries, and I had put money into retirement savings and thought everything was going to be fine, that I'd be fairly comfortable in my old age.

That was until one day my brother in-law said to me; "y'know the average white collar worker is living 'til 85 today, and by the time we get there, who knows what it'll be, maybe 95, 105 - can you afford to fund it?"

I thought, that's very interesting, I never really looked that closely at it, I just assumed I was in good shape. So, I went and looked at it, crunched the numbers, noticed that fund performance had been very poor over the previous decade and decided that I was not going to be able to enjoy the kind of lifestyle I would like in my retirement.

So, I thought, okay, I need to find an alternative. I don't know what it is, but I need to find it. So I started applying the techniques, and almost immediately I got invited to join a business networking group by one of my clients.

There was a member of that business networking site who had bought a premium package which enabled them to e-mail everybody in the network. And so I got an e-mail from this chap, you can look him up actually, his name is Andy Shaw, and he has a book called *Get Your Money for Nothing and Your Property for Free*, which is a take on the title of a Dire Straits song from the '80s.

This intrigued me, it was £20 to buy the book, and I thought, worst case: I've wasted £20. So I bought it and it talked about how to buy houses for below their market value, refurbish them, then rent them out, and then refinance them to get your money back and do it again.

I thought, what a genius plan. So I cashed in everything, including all my stock options and employee stockholdings, took equity out of the family home and started buying rental properties. I'm not really recommending that book for today's market but it served its purpose for me at the time.

Now, if and when I ever do retire, given that I really love what I do and am not inclined to give it up any time soon, I'm pretty sure I'm going to be okay. So, this is how you can apply these principles to everyday situations where you need to.

Again, the solution came not by some wave of a magic wand but my taking action on the physical plane with definiteness of purpose.

Of course, I do this not just for myself, but for some clients as well. I'll just give you a couple of real examples here of how it's worked.

Joanna

Joanna was a lady who had taken time out to have and raise a child, but had unfortunately separated from her husband, and didn't know what to do with her life. She had an idea of what she wanted but lacked a clear vision and plan of action.

By applying the principles I taught her she was able to generate a new career in a holistic field. She contacted me a year after she finished her program with me to tell me how well she was doing. Quite incredible considering that until she applied these principles she had spent a lot of time going in circles and getting nowhere.

Paul

Paul, a lovely fellow from The Netherlands, who was living in the U.K., and had what he called 'a feeling of restlessness'. He would get a very strong sensation in his chest, a kind of anxiety, when he went into new situations.

We worked hard to reduce that, and get rid of it and discovered what was causing it – he actually had a deep desire to return to his homeland, but was denying it, stuffing it down because he couldn't see how to make it possible. His unconscious mind was making him feel uncomfortable so he'd get the message.

Once we got that to the level of conscious awareness we were able to release it and get clarity around what would really make him happy. What he really wanted to do was have a semi-self-sufficient kind of community style of living in a farmhouse, near the sea, with a couple or three families living there and growing their own food as much as they could.

As soon as he started applying these principles, his sister, who happened to be living in such a farmhouse, decided she wanted to move back into the city and offered him a place to live there, rent-free. What a coincidence!

Of course, one challenge for him was that his wife, who was a personal assistant, was wondering how she was going to earn a living in The Netherlands. It turns out, at that time, she came across the concept of 'virtual assistant', where she can have clients she can serve from anywhere, doing it virtually.

How interesting that all these things came to light when he started applying the principles. He said that the turning point for him was when he created and started using his **HEART Manifesto**.

Elisabeth

Now, I'd also like to tell you about Elisabeth. She would admit her life was a mess. She was exhausted all the time, always ill and in pain. She wanted to leave her relationship but she was afraid she couldn't support herself. Her dream was to emigrate to New Zealand, which she had visited and fallen in love with.

She wanted to live there, do holistic work, and swim with the dolphins. But she had no job, no money, no sponsor and couldn't see how it was possible.

Anyway, once we repaired her energy system and released the hidden blocks, we created a **HEART Manifesto** for her and applied the exercises. Incredibly, for the past three years, she has been living her dream life in New Zealand, helping young recovering addicts rehabilitate.

And best of all, she can swim with dolphins whenever she likes. And that's simply because she chose, at that time, to apply these basic principles which I'm going to tell you about shortly.

Dean

Dean is a young man from the U.K. who was at rock bottom. His relationships were a disaster, his job no longer served him, he had low self-esteem and confidence, suffered from anxiety and overwhelm, was prone to binge eating on junk food and felt that life was passing him by.

By using these principles he gained a new sense of self belief, enthusiasm and energy for life again, started a fitness regime, gained confidence, started his own online business and runs a networking group with people who are looking to make changes to create healthier, joy-filled lives with plenty of freedom. Dean is now doing what he loves and loving what he does.

OK, these examples are all well and good, but how do you make it work for yourself? Let's get into that in the following sections.

Chapter 6: Keys to Success

What does it all this mean? What does it boil down to? Basically, there is a thing called the Quantum Field, there is an immutable law of the Universe called the Law of Attraction, that human energy affects matter, and human thoughts shape reality.

"There is a Quantum Field, there's a Law of Attraction, human energy affects matter, human thoughts shape reality."

I just thought that needed repeating.

We can also see that emotions have a role to play, as does taking action. We know that thoughts and the words that express those thoughts are important in setting up a vibration in our energy field that turns us into little magnets, attracting whatever we are currently resonating with.

So, putting it all together we can summarize the keys to success thus:

• **The power of the word**. You need to express yourself verbally to set up the vibration of what you want to achieve.

• **Clarity**. You need to be clear about what you want. If you can't make your mind up, the universe, being infinitely patient, will happily wait for you to do that. In this lifetime, or the next, or the one after that.

• **Belief**. Your belief in it is key. What you believe, is. Whether these beliefs are conscious or unconscious. With your beliefs, you are making your reality.

- **Doing it without ego**. That is, not because you want to change the world, not because you want to keep up or be better than the Joneses. It has to be from the heart.

- **Doing it with emotion or feeling**. Human emotions are key to manifesting success.

- **Taking action**. You have to take action in the physical world. As I said before, you can't just 'ohm' things into existence.

Let's say I was out driving in the countryside somewhere, and I noticed that my fuel tank was empty. What am I going to do? Am I going to make a picture of a full fuel tank, maybe stick it onto the display, light an incense stick and put that on the dashboard, just go 'ohhhmmmm, ahhhh, my tank is full, my tank is full' – is it going to fill up like that? No, I don't think so either.

What I'm going to do is look for a service station. Maybe I'm in the middle of nowhere and there aren't any gas stations, but as soon as I set my intention, I know I'm going to find one. And, most likely, it's been there for years, even if I've never noticed it before.

Another thing to be aware of is **consistency**. We have to do it all the time, and be consistent about what we're doing. So many people give up right before the point of breakthrough. Stick with it. It must work. It is a law of nature.

Finally, I have found that an **attitude of gratitude** helps considerably. When you see miserable people walking around, what do they get in their life? Yup, more things to be miserable about.

So when you have a sense of gratitude and thankfulness, what are you going to get in your life? More things to be thankful for. If you get nothing else out of this book, at least take that away. You may even find that this single key delivers even greater result that you imagined.

So, how do you make it work for you? I'm going to show you how to do it with a method that I've had numerous examples of success with - both for myself and many others.

Chapter 7: Create Your HEART Manifesto

The HEART Manifesto

As soon as I learned about how we create our reality every day, mostly unconsciously, I set about discovering the metaphysical principles and natural processes that enable it to happen.

Using the skills developed over decades as a communications professional in the technology industry I set about condensing these complex concepts into an easy-to-use tool. I have honed it over 11 years; I have researched it, applied it, tweaked it, built upon it with learnings, from studying I've done and real world practice with myself and my clients.

I've come up with a <u>proven</u> methodology called the HEART Manifesto. And now, it's time for you to create your own. I have broken it down into segments to show you how it builds and will put it all together for you at the end of the section.

As I said earlier, if you go to the web page – <u>http://www.academy4empowerment.com/heart-manifesto</u> - and sign up for the video tutorial that this book complements, as described in the Introduction, you can download a workbook that will help you get a clear picture of what you want plus a blank form to fill in to make it even easier for you to create your own **HEART Manifesto**.

This is how it works:

The Declaration

As I have explained, words are important; we start off with the words, and the first part of it is a declaration. To start, we declare "*Dear...*"

Then we have to decide who or what we are addressing. I write in here "*Dear Universe,*" but you can put anything you want. You can put "*Dear God*", "*Dear Angels*", "*Dear Spirit*", "*Dear Quantum Field*", or you could just put "*Dear Self*" if your belief system doesn't support any of those things; whatever feels appropriate for you.

It doesn't really matter what you call it, so long as it represents the highest good that you can envisage. It's your intention that's important.

Then, we write "*I declare my will*", which is us stating to ourselves that this is our declaration, that it is not some wimpy prayer; it's recognition that we are in control and creating our own reality.

Now we put "*to rinse away the old me*" – that's just giving the intention that we want to change, to release things which have been holding us back, and get them out of the way. I often say to people it's good to do this in the shower, because then, as well as metaphorically rinsing away the old you, you are literally rinsing yourself, and that reinforces it.

Water is energetically and metaphysically purifying as well as physically. And also, as a liquid, it's somewhere between ether and solid, so it's actually a medium for making the unmanifest manifest. If that makes sense. You don't need to worry about all of that, just follow the plan, and it works anyway.

So the next bit is to *"rise above the constraints of this Earth plane"*, recognizing that in the physical world we have perceived constraints. However, we don't have to be constrained by them, because we are the masters of our universe and we can change that. I'm not saying you can break the laws of physics, I'm just saying we need to release the artificial constraints that we have imposed upon ourselves.

And then we say *"and to step into the highest level of my contract"*. This is an acknowledgement that maybe we've come here to do something in this lifetime, we have some purpose to our existence, an agreement of some kind that we want to honor. So, we put it in here as a reminder of that.

And then we say *"so that I may be of the greatest possible service"*. If, like me, you are called to serve, you are in the right place. This is a place for Light Workers, it's our job to help people to make a difference in the world. And I know that's you, or you wouldn't be reading this in the first place.

So then add *"to you"* that is, the Universe or whomever you've written at the top of the page, *"to myself, to my family"*, and by family we mean, not just physical relatives on the physical plane, but also our spiritual family: the angels, the guides, whatever you want to call them, that support us in our existence, who we are reunited with when we return to the non-physical.

And also, *"and all human kind"*, so reinforcing we're people that really think we can, know we can, and want to make a difference in the world.

The Turnaround

So the second stanza, or paragraph, is called 'the Turnaround', and it's about forgiveness and gratitude because forgiveness is the key to healing, and gratitude is the key to manifesting.

So we start off with *"I forgive my father/mother/husband/wife/partner/significant other"*; put their names in; *"brothers, sisters,"* put their names in, *"sons, daughters"*, any offspring you may have, put their names in, also put cousins, aunts, uncles, put their names in. Even if you think there's nothing to forgive, put their name in anyway.

Your boss, if you have one, your teacher, any authority figures in your life. Put in any neighbors, people in shops you may know, colleagues, and anyone else who you think may have done you wrong: put all their names in.

As you do this, and as you're saying it out loud to yourself every day, other people will come to mind who you have not thought of here. Let them come up, and let them go. And that's all there is to it.

And then we say *"I thank them for playing their parts perfectly, in helping me learn my life lesson"*.

Forgiveness is very important. Let's suppose someone has wronged you. I've worked with people who have been abused, and people who have all kinds of other issues, and the most important learning is this: if you're holding resentment, anger, hatred, whatever, any kind of negative emotions against these people, who does it actually hurt?

Is it hurting them? Do they even know you harbor it? If they did, would they even care?

The point is this: the only person it hurts is you. So you have to let it go, we have to go through some kind of forgiveness process. It doesn't mean we condone what they did, it just means we no longer need to endure the negative emotions associated with it.

I have seen it so many times where a resentment eats away at a person over years and they inevitably end up with some undesirable consequence, such as a serious disease. So it is really important to practice forgiveness on a daily basis until we can really feel it in our hearts.

And then, in terms of thanking them for playing their parts, this is more of a metaphysical concept. It works on the philosophy that we incarnate in many lifetimes for learning and soul growth.

Between lives, we plan out our lifetimes to some extent – I think we still have a certain amount of free will, but there are some milestones that we have to hit – and if we are to get a particular learning in this lifetime, we need other people to incarnate with us to help give us that.

And especially, when it's a really big one, we might ask ourselves, who loves us enough to come down to Earth at this time with us, and be so terrible to us, to give us such a fantastic opportunity for learning and growth? Now, I know that's going to be a stretch for some people, but I entreat you to think about it. It can make quite a difference if you can look at things differently.

Even if you're not buying it, do it anyway because this is a sound process that works when it is applied consistently.

The Desire

The final stanza is called 'The Desire', and we start off with repeating "*I declare my will*", that's to remind us again that we are, in fact, in charge here. Then we need to tailor it to your particular need - what is your desire?

"*To be in a healthy body*", I always put that. I get quite a few people coming to me with quite serious conditions, and even if you don't have anything at the moment that you would consider an ailment of any kind, it's always good to put this in as a reminder.

We say "*to be in a close, loving relationship with* ___", and you put in the name of your beloved. Or, if you don't have one, you can put "*my ideal partner*". If you really do not want a close relationship at this time, then just leave it out.

And then you can say "*to be in a career that* ___". So, for example, "*to be in a career that uses my creativity and compassion to help people lead the life they were born to lead*". That might be something like what I would put, or I could put something more specific like, "*to be a holistic practitioner*", something like that. Be specific to what you want to do with your days.

Remember this - the way to earn good money in the world today is by providing value and being rewarded for it. So to be clear, I am not advocating just sitting down and reciting these words - you will have to take action as well, so make sure it is something that you love and are inspired to do.

Moving on, then you can insert any other desires, like "*to have a four bedroom house in the country up a hill with a drive*" or "*to *have a green car that I can get the whole family and the dog in"*, anything like that – anything at all, don't hold back.

And then finally, we finish it off with *"and have all the abundance that I so thoroughly deserve"*. I put that in, because, in my experience, lack of self-worth is one of the major blocks that people have to manifesting, but as human angels who have come down to help facilitate massive planetary change, we are the exalted ones.

The angels worship us, so any feelings you have about not being worthy - put them away because it's just nonsense.

Another thing I often hear is, "if I have more it's taking it away from somebody else". But, come on guys, the universe is infinitely abundant, it's all energy. Everything is energy. There's always more energy and there's more than enough for everybody to have everything they want. The only thing stopping us is our own self-limiting beliefs.

So get with it. And besides, who does it serve for you to stay poor? Imagine what you could do if you were wealthy. You can't be a philanthropist if you don't have any money, and money is just another form of energy.

To clarify again, I'm not saying focus on the money, I'm saying focus on what you want. Money is only valuable for what it can buy, so focus on what you want and put aside any thoughts that you don't deserve it anyway.

Remember, it will come through the normal machinations of the world and possibly in ways that you couldn't imagine, not necessarily through having funds to purchase it.

The Closing

Then we do The Closing, and it's simply; "*and so it is, and so it is, and so it is*". And that's just reinforcing that this is in the present. Remember, we want to set up the vibration that what we're looking for already is. We want to create the state of **being**, not the state of **wanting**, which would leave us forever **wanting** and never **having** our desires.

The Tool

And so, that basically is the bones of the tool. And it looks a bit like this when it's written out in full. As I said, you'll find a worksheet on the website where you can adapt it to your own use. So:

Dear Universe,

I declare my will to rinse away the old me, to rise above the constraints of this Earth plain, and step into the highest level of my contract so that I may be of the greatest possible service to you, myself, my family and all human kind.

I forgive __ (enter everyone's names)______, and anyone else who I perceive may have wronged me. I thank them for playing their parts perfectly in helping me learn my life lesson.

I declare my will to be in a healthy body, to be in a close loving relationship with my ideal partner, to be in a career that allows to me to express myself creatively, helps others and brings me joy __ (or whatever you want from your career or the way you will deliver value)__, and to have all the abundance that I so thoroughly deserve (and put in any other things that you want in your life at this time).

And so it is. And so it is. And so it is.

And this is something you need to say out loud every single day. But, only once a day is enough for you. Just saying it won't be enough on its own, though. Read on to unleash the real power of this amazing tool.

True mastery of the Law of Attraction: do it with **HEART**.

Chapter 8: Do It With HEART

Do it with HEART

I talked in Chapter 6 about the keys to success. And the real key is to do it with HEART. Now this is a mnemonic I've created to turn what was otherwise just an affirmation, into a powerful metaphysical tool.

The mnemonic is a simple way to remember what the keys to unlocking the power of the Universe are and to help you stay on track when applying these principles.

So, what does **HEART** stand for?

H = Heart. What that means is, do it from the heart. Without ego, without judgment. Totally non-judgmentally. Can you do that? Yes you can, and it's important that you do.

E = Emotion. We've talked quite a bit about putting feeling into it, and this may be the most important point. Those things that you're looking for in the third stanza of those words - how does it feel to have those already? What would it feel like if you already had them in your life? That's the feeling you're trying to get. You've got to bring the emotion to it, and you've got to put it into the words when you say it. This is a critical key to success.

A = Action. You've got to take action. We've talked about this: take every reasonable step every day. Abraham, via Esther Hicks, says **"it is the action you take today that ties you to the future outcome"**. Anyone who knows anything about this stuff knows you have got to take action. You cannot 'ohm' it into existence.

R = Repetition. This means repeat it **constantly**, every day. Maybe in the shower, maybe not. But, it also means do it **consistently**, sticking with what you want, not changing your mind all the time, and doing it daily. That's what repetition is about, so make sure you do that.

T = Thankfulness. Adopt an attitude of gratitude to attract more things to be thankful for. Practice gratitude for everything in your life and every experience you have, no matter how mundane, and watch how your world magically transforms into one of wonder.

Go back to the words, when you do write them out in your worksheet, read your manifesto again with emotion. How does it make you feel? Does it excite and inspire you? Does it make you happy? Then, it will work.

If not, then there is something missing - check out the next chapter to find whether you need one more piece to complete your puzzle.

Chapter 9: What's Next?

If when you read your **HEART Manifesto** out loud and put the emotion into it, it feels like there is something missing, or it doesn't really inspire and excite you, then you may need to take one more step to tap into its power.

Perhaps you are not really clear on what you want? Maybe your goals are 'away-from' rather than 'towards' goals - i.e. you are focusing in what you don't want, and will surely get more of that.

Or could you have negative emotions, limiting beliefs or other mental/emotional blocks that may be slowing you down, getting in the way or stopping you from having what you desire?

If you are experiencing high levels of stress, unwarranted or inappropriate negative emotions such as anger, sadness, fear, hurt and guilt, or have major physical world challenges like lots of clutter, email backlogs or such an overwhelming number of tasks that you never make progress on anything, then you might need a little help to clear these up before being able to fully utilize the power of the Universe.

You may need to release limiting beliefs including some unconscious ones you don't even know about. Also, you may want to raise your vibration – we haven't talked about that much here – but if you can avoid things that bring your vibration down, and do more things which raise it up, you will actually have a lot more success with creating your ideal life.

You can find an excellent tutorial on how to raise your vibration - essentially increase your 'Quantum Energy Quotient' - on my website www.academy4empowerment.com. It is right on the home page and it's called *Step Into Your Power.*

BlockBuster Session

So, with those things in mind, to thank you for taking the time to read this book and to put into practice my teachings here, I'm going to offer you a free **BlockBuster Session** with me. This will be up to 30 minutes by Skype, VSee or telephone, wherever you are in the world (or you can phone me if you want).

Just go to www.academy4empowerment.com/heart-manifesto and sign up for the **HEART Manifesto tutorial**, remembering to enter the coupon code "manifest now" to get your 100% discount when you check out.

You will get the hour or so long video and the workbook already mentioned in these pages, but more importantly you will get an email inviting you to book your **BlockBuster Session** with me.

And for so long as I can handle the demand, I will do this. We'll blow out the major barrier to your success; be it a limiting belief, emotion, etc. And give you some information on how to keep your vibration up. Wouldn't that be cool? Sign up for the tutorial now and look out for the e-mail.

Finally, if you do want to delve further into this, I have included a bibliography at the end to reference the books and websites that I talked about in this book.

With your own Googling and library access, you can certainly look even further into it, but I have read so many books, gone to so many workshops and so many courses, spent tens of thousands on training, plus countless hours experimenting on myself and clients, then and boiled it all down to this, so that you don't have to.

But if you want to, these are some good starting points.

So it just remains to be said: thank you very much for taking the time. I hope you feel more empowered, more awakened, and looking forward to achieving greater success in your personal life and your business life and in helping others. Now is the time to use the **HEART Manifesto** to master the Law of Attraction, create the massive success you were born to enjoy and make a huge contribution to the world.

Together we can change the planet for the better, so thank you.

Shine On!

Bibliography

1. *The Divine Matrix*, Gregg Braden, Hay House Inc, 2007, ISBN 978-1-4019-0573-6

2. *Stop the Excuses: How to Change Lifelong Thoughts*, Dr Wayne Dyer, Hay House Inc, 2009, ISBN 978-1-84850-027-3

3. *E-Squared*, Pam Grout, Hay House Inc, 2013, ISBN 978-1-4019-3890-1

4. *A Dynamical Theory of the Electromagnetic Field*, J Clerk Maxwell, Royal Society Publishing, 1864

5. *The Biology of Belief*, Bruce H Lipton PhD, Hay House Inc, 2005, ISBN 978-1-4019-2312-9

6. *Science and the Akashic Field: An Integral Theory of Everything*, Ervin Lazlo, Inner Traditions, 2nd Edition 2010, ISBN 1594771812

7. *Prayers of the Cosmos: Meditations on the Aramaic Words of Jesus*, Neil Douglas-Klotz, HarperOne, 2009, ISBN-13: 978-0060619954

8. *The Isaiah Effect*, Gregg Braden, Hay House Inc, 2005, ISBN-13: 978-1591793045

9. *The Power of Awareness*, Neville Goddard, Martino Fine Books, 2009 (original 1952), ISBN-13: 978-1578988471

10. *The Secret*, Rhonda Byrne, Simon & Schuster, 2006, ISBN-13: 978-1847370297

11. *The Science of Getting Rich*, Wallace Wattles, http://www.soilandhealth.org/03sov/0304spiritpsych/030412.Wattle.Getting.Rich.pdf

12. *Think and Grow Rich*, Napoleon Hill, http://freepdfs.org/pdf/think-grow-rich

13. *Zorba the Greek*, Nikos Kazantzakis, Faber & Faber, 2008 (original 1946), ISBN-13: 978-0571241705

For More Information

Academy 4 Empowerment

Keith Corbett is the founder of Academy 4 Empowerment - www.academy4empowerment.com - an informational and educational resource for awakening entrepreneurs.

As a teacher, author and inspirational speaker, he shows them how to harness the natural laws of the Universe and tap into their own inner brilliance to achieve the massive success they were born for.

Woodland Wellness

Keith Corbett is also proprietor of Woodland Wellness - www.woodlandwellness.co.uk- a holistic healing arts practice based in Staffordshire, UK and serving clients worldwide. He specializes in natural healing for Chronic Reversed Polarity, being the only certified European practitioner using the Keith Smith Reversal Method.